Original title: Poesia's Prism

Author: Liina Liblikas
Editor: Jessica Elisabeth Luik
ISBN 978-9916-39-473-1

Poesia's Prism

Liina Liblikas

Lyrical Lavaliere

Around thy neck, a silken thread,
Bearing a charm, so light it treads.
A pendant whispers, secrets to keep,
In every fold, where shadows creep.

A harmony clasped with tender care,
Each gem a note in the evening's air.
The moon observes with a lustrous gaze,
As stars adorn the night's necklace lace.

In the ballroom of the twilight hours,
Where dreams are worn and hope empowers.
The lyrical lavaliere, a dancer's prize,
Moves to the rhythm that in slumber lies.

Encircling warmth, a soft embrace,
A symphony held in a lover's space.
With each heartbeat, a melody rare,
In the lyrical lavaliere, life's flair.

Rhapsodic Radiance

In effervescent hues, the dawn is painted,
A rhapsodic radiance, by night untainted.
A canvas vast, with colors spun,
Announcing the arrival of the sun.

The sky, a stage for light's ballet,
Where clouds in pastel costumes sway.
Each ray a measure in a silent score,
A brilliant crescendo of the day in store.

Birdsong weaves through the vibrant gleam,
A natural chorus by the morning stream.
Flowers awaken in rhapsodies bright,
Their faces turned to embrace the light.

With every hour, the splendor grows,
In a symphony of shades, the sunset shows.
When dusk arrives in a tranquil dance,
The rhapsodic radiance takes one last glance.

Illuminated Intonations

Upon the stage of twilight's gleam,
Where shadows dance and poets dream,
Each whispered verse a shining ray,
Illuminating thoughts that stray.

The metered truths in darkness found,
As heartfelt echoes softly sound,
Intonations cast their spell,
In every syllable, they dwell.

Through radiant prose, the night's adorned,
With stanzas bright, the black is scorned,
Illuminating with each line,
Where words and brilliance intertwine.

Melodic Chroma

In the orchestra of light,
Colors play with pure delight,
Notes of red and blue combine,
In a symphony divine.

A canvas vast as sound is deep,
Brushstrokes in a rhythmic sweep,
Melodies in hues that bleed,
Chromatic scales that souls can read.

Vibrant tints in harmony,
Compose the world's rare melody,
Each pigment a song, a sonic bloom,
In the concert hall's grand room.

Diction in Indigo

Underneath the indigo skies,
Where velvet nightfall softly lies,
Words emerge with deep precision,
Crafting dreams with clear vision.

Sentences in sapphire flows,
Conveying thoughts in twilight glows,
In ink-dipped lines, they calmly wait,
Expressions rich that resonate.

A lexicon in darkest blue,
Where every metaphor rings true,
The prose that fills the night so wide,
In indigo, they confide.

Phrases in Pigment

With palette full and brush in hand,
The artist writes across the land,
Each stroke a word, a vibrant phrase,
A pigment poem of endless days.

In colors bold, the lines take flight,
From morning's gold to deepest night,
The syntax in each shade differs,
A chromatic script that whispers.

Upon the earthen parchment spread,
The painted adjectives are shed,
In sentences of green and brown,
The artist's verses claim renown.

Ballad of Brilliance

In realms of endless diamond skies,
With stars that dance and softly glint,
The moon does rise, her watchful eyes,
Over dreams that lovers print.

Upon the canvas of the night,
Each gleam tells stories old and true,
A bard sings of the valiant knight,
And love that springs like morning dew.

The brilliance of a hopeful heart,
Through trials that test and times that try,
Kindles courage to impart,
The strength to soar, the will to fly.

In the Ballad of Brilliance bright,
Echoes of valor gently sway,
Inspiring all souls to light,
Their way toward the break of day.

Hue Haiku Harmony

Crimson sunset glow,
Canvas kissed by nature's brush,
Evening's soft embrace.

Verdant forest shade,
Whispering leaves tell their tales,
Nature's hushed secrets.

Azure ocean depth,
Waves in rhythmic harmonies,
Salted air, serene.

Golden daffodils,
Trumpets heralding the spring,
Sun's warmth awakens.

Coloratura of Couplets

Lifted high on wings of song,
Her voice cascades, pure and strong.

Pierces through the sullen sky,
Where lower notes dare not fly.

Each note a vibrant, joyous leap,
Weaving dreams that banish sleep.

The coloratura's trills and flights,
Adorn the silent air of nights.

Tinged Thoughts

Shadows paint the corners of my mind,
Tinged with thoughts of hues undefined.
Glimmers of the past tender and kind,
On the canvas of my memory signed.

A spectrum of emotions deeply lined,
In each shade, a story intertwined.
Whispers of time forever wind,
Through heartstrings that softly bind.

Sunset's blush fades into night,
Borrowed colors retreat from sight.
Yet in dreams, they find new height,
Resurrecting day with gentle light.

Vibrant Versification

In the orchard where the sunlight dances,
Beneath the boughs where fragrant winds play,
Nature's hues in radiant stanzas,
Kiss the soul with warmth of May.

Awakened blooms of bright persuasion,
Tendrils twisting turning tight,
Each petal a word in floral equation,
Verses of day dissolving night.

Butterflies in airy flutters,
Whispering secrets, verse so sweet,
Over blooms their wingtips mutter,
Poems in motion, nature's feat.

Metrical Mosaic

Words like tiles in patterns binding,
Woven tales in rhythm tight,
Every line and phrase is finding,
Place and time in metered light.

Stanzas set in structured order,
Skies of prose on parchment laid,
Phrases cut as from recorder,
Images in ink arrayed.

Narratives in colored pieces,
Broken, reformed, a tale anew,
Textured tones that never ceases,
A tapestried lore of countless hue.

Tinted Translations

Whispered words in tongues of olden,
Scripted shadows that tales convey,
Ancient stories, colors golden,
In modern minds find place to stay.

Glimpses through the stained glass stories,
Light in spectrums, speech revealed,
Past and present in allegories,
Pigmented paragraphs unsealed.

All the world's a canvas broad,
Where every shade's a word so dear,
Each brushstroke is a silent laud,
A vibrant voice we see more than hear.

Synesthetic Strophes

Verse that tingles on the tongue's tip,
Taste of tangerine and rhyme,
Syntax swirled with sense’s grip,
Synesthetic beats in time.

Chromatic chords in meter melting,
Poetry in palette's pride,
Resonant hues our hearts are felt in,
Stanzas where senses collide.

Touch the texture of the tune,
Words woven in aural array,
Sentence sounds that croon and croon,
A symphony of synesthesia's play.

Spectrum in Strophes

Colors dance in spectral glow,
Every hue a unique flow,
Threads of light finely woven,
Nature’s kaleidoscopic token.

Red whispers tales of fervent love,
Orange radiates warmth from above,
Yellow shines like morning’s bloom,
Green tells of life in endless loom.

Indigo dreams of the deep night sky,
Violet whispers a gentle lullaby,
Ribboned rainbow across the view,
Spectrum’s gift in vivid hue.

Azure Alliterations

Azure skies in ample arch,
Alluring as the larks embark.
Amethyst aligned afar,
Alliance 'twixt the sun and star.

Alabaster clouds afloat,
Abandoning their airy boat.
Across the azure, they ascend,
Aloft to where the colors blend.

Alight with dreams, they drift away,
Ascend into the break of day.
Azure whispers to the wind,
Allure that in the sky is pinned.

Mauve Moods and Melodies

Mauve moods meld with the falling night,
Melodies meander in leisured flight.
Mystic shades merge in the dusky dome,
Moonlit sonatas softly roam.

Moments marinated in muted hue,
Musical whispers, and thoughts anew.
Musing minds meander through dreams,
Mixing memory in pensive streams.

Modest mauve, a muse for the heart,
Motifs murmuring a quiet start.
Mellowed tunes in the twilight weave,
Mauve moods and melodies at eve.

Aquarelle Quatrains

Watercolor wonders softly seep,
Layered lightness, brushstrokes deep.
A canvas kissed by liquid shade,
In aquarelle quatrains arrayed.

Cerulean blues with touches of cream,
Pigments pooling in a dream.
Pastel visions lightly drawn,
Dawn's palette from the palette born.

Dappled days dip into the brush,
Hues hush the world into a blush.
Quatrains composed in water’s flow,
Aquarelle’s art, a tranquil show.

Alabaster Allusions

Whispered tales in hues so pale,
Alabaster secrets unveil.
Ghostly whispers in the breeze,
Allusions formed to softly tease.

Echoes dance in stilly night,
Underneath the moon's soft light.
Carving shadows, telling tales,
Silent songs that love regales.

In the calm, an ivory swath,
Thoughts adrift on alabaster path.
Fragile hopes with tender gleams,
Woven tight in dreams' soft seams.

Lines in Lavender

Lavender strokes on the canvas of dusk,
Skies painted with evening's tender musk.
A tapestry woven with twilight's own hand,
Where day's rosy hues meet night's quiet band.

Fields of lavender sway in repose,
Whispers of calm where serenity grows.
Each blossom penned in nature's own script,
A symphony in lilac, delicately tipped.

Dreams sketched in lines of muted hue,
Where peace resides and hearts renew.
In lavender shades, the world softens its view,
While life's vivid colors merge and construe.

Prosaic Prismatica

In mundane moments, colors blend,
Through prosaic glass, light bends.
Prismatic views of everyday,
Spin the common in a gracious way.

Daily deeds refract anew,
In splendid shades of varied hue.
Prismatica of the mind,
Garnishes the dull, the undefined.

Colors cast on walls of thought,
Prosaic patterns finely wrought.
Life seen through a different lens,
With prismatica the grayness ends.

Garnished in Green

Emerald whispers in the wind,
Nature's own vigorously penned.
The verdant robe of earthen wear,
Exuberance in the air we share.

Canopies printed in chlorophyll dyes,
Where the rustle of life never dies.
Garnished in green, the world is seen,
A realm alive, eternally keen.

Fields and forests, a verdurous scene,
Infinite shades of vibrant green.
Life's lush tapestry, so serene,
Is garnished with beauty, a living dream.

Gilded Garnet Lyrics

In depths of earth where dark does reign,
Garnet glistens like a haunting strain.
Its hue, a tale of silent might,
A gilded song in the absence of light.

Against the forge, it dances bright,
Alive with fiery, inner light.
A thread of scarlet, a sunset’s kiss,
In every facet, an artist's bliss.

Whispers of history within its gleam,
A gem that fuels the dreamer’s dream.
Its ruby choir sings beneath the loam,
In earthen crypts where treasure roams.

Amber Ambience Verses

Suspended time in golden glow,
Amber whispers ancient flow.
Resin tears that trees did weep,
Now in honeyed silence steep.

Caught within its tawny hue,
Life from a time we never knew.
Insects held in sweet repose,
Nature's art that time chose.

Through this window of the past,
We glimpse moments that forever last.
A warm ambience, a captured sun,
An epoch's end, a new day begun.

Scarlet Scansion

Scarlet echoes on the wall,
A poet's heart, a lover’s call.
Each strophe laced with passion's hue,
A scansion painted through and through.

Verses carved in crimson deep,
A fiery soul that does not sleep.
Rhythmic beats in sanguine spread,
With every line, emotion fed.

Scarlet ink on parchment pale,
A narrative of love’s grand tale.
Through metered heartbeats, tender, raw,
The scarlet scansion of life's awe.

Pastel Prose Poems

Words whispered in pastel tones,
Softly they speak, as if through stones.
Gentle hues of written prose,
Where the quiet thought quite clearly shows.

A canvas painted with language light,
Colors converge in the reader's sight.
Each verse a brushstroke, gentle, demure,
In the world of prose, pastels endure.

Lilac whispers, minty dreams,
Each line a part of the painter's schemes.
The prose that wears a tranquil face,
In delicate words, one finds grace.

Topaz Tercets

In fields of gold, the topaz shines,
Etched in earth, where sunlight dines.
Nature's gem, a beacon bright,
Illuminating dusky night.

Flame incarnate, fire's child,
Gift of warmth, tempered wild.
Captured essence of the day,
In crystal bounds, it dares to stay.

Ancient relic, history's eye,
Whispering tales of the sky.
Jeweled testament, regal and bold,
Within its facets, stories told.

Scribe in Spectrum Light

Under a prism's gentle thrall,
The scribe pens tales that gently call.
A spectrum dance upon the wall,
As ink and colors interweave and enthrall.

With quill that trails a rainbow hue,
The parchment breathes in shades anew.
Words emerge in chromatic view,
A symphony in every stroke, ever true.

Fingers stained in polychrome dreams,
Indenting texture, patterned themes.
Light weaves silence into streams,
Scribing fantasies in spectrum beams.

Opus in Ochre

Upon a canvas, stark and bare,
An artist's soul laid open, there.
The ochre bleeds from deep within,
Each stroke a verse, a love affair.

In earthen tones, the painter's hands
Compose the heart of arid lands.
The dusky pigment tells its tales,
In opus grand, the artwork stands.

A symphony in muted gold,
The ochre's story, bravely told.
Each brush a line, a life unfolds,
On canvas vast, the vision's bold.

Periwinkle Poetics

Shades of periwinkle spread across the sky,
Soothing the horizon where the sparrows fly.
In each gentle hue, a poem's soft embrace,
Enshrouding the world in a whimsical lace.

Unfurling its color at dusk and at dawn,
The periwinkle whispers the day is reborn.
Its verses enchanter, in twilight's last gleam,
Casting through the night, a poet's silent dream.

A tapestry woven with threads of light blue,
Each knot is a word, and each stitch something true.
Through periwinkle poetics, the mind's canvas fills,
In the quiet deepening, inspiration distills.

The Rainbow Scribe

In hues of seven, the sky was drawn,
A canvas wide for the scribe's yawn.
The drizzle's kiss and sun's gentle bribe,
Birthed arcs of color, a chromatic tribe.

With quill of light and spectrum wide,
The scribe inscribes on the azure tide.
Each droplet a word on nature's page,
Tales of the sun and storm's soft rage.

The curve of joy in celestial sprawl,
A signature of peace above us all.
The rainbow scribe, both end and start,
Penning hope within the human heart.

Stanzaic Splendor

Upon the parchment of the day,
Words dance in verse, in array.
Stanzas crafted with careful splendor,
Echoing thoughts tender and tender.

The poet weaves a silent song,
A tapestry where rhymes belong.
Each line a thread, a story spun,
Under the watchful eye of the sun.

Symphony in silence, rhythm in space,
Verse carries the heart at a tranquil pace.
In the splendor of stanzaic form,
Feelings are harnessed, and dreams are born.

Refracted Dreams

In slumber’s keep, where dreams are stitched,
Refracted through the mind's rich loom.
A tapestry of desire, anxiety switched,
Into realms where ideas bloom.

Each dream, a ray of hope or fear,
Bending through the psyche's prism.
A spectrum of emotions, crystal clear,
Within the subconscious chasm.

Chasing shadows within the night,
We swim in pools of fantasy’s light.
Refracted dreams, with colors rife,
Warp and weft the threads of life.

Lyric Luminescence

In the quiet before dawn's gleam,
There whispers a melody, a soft stream.
Notes like starlight, gently unfurl,
Lyric luminescence in the waking world.

Each word a pulse of light in the void,
Poetry's glow, in darkness deployed.
Verses sparking the air, igniting thought,
The luminescence of lyrics sought.

The beat of the heart, the breath of night,
In concert with words that take flight.
Illuminate the soul with each cadence,
A symphony of luminous resonance.

Cobalt Cadences

In depths of azure dreams, I dive,
Submerged in cobalt tone,
Each wave a stanza, clear and alive,
The ocean's pulse, its own.

Two shades collide in silent dance,
A myriad of hues,
In fleeting, swirling, deep expanse,
Their whispering my muse.

The midnight sky joins in the choir,
A sapphire symphony,
Stars dotting measures, sparks of fire,
In ink-blue harmony.

In cobalt cadences, I sail,
With breezes soft as lace,
Adrift upon a timeless tale,
Embraced in indigo's grace.

Whispered Wavelengths

Soft hums of hushed vibrations stirred,
A secret speech, unseen,
Transmitted without need for word,
In spaces in between.

The tender rustle of the leaves,
A murmur through the trees,
Unspoken thoughts that night conceives,
Carried on a breeze.

Beneath the silent surface hides,
A chorus in the light,
Resonating, it provides,
Whispered wavelengths of the night.

In quietude, these unheard notes,
Compose the earth's soft song,
A melody that gently floats,
And carries us along.

Radiant Rhythms

With each sunrise, the world's reborn,
The sky alight with grace,
With radiant rhythms of the morn,
A new day we embrace.

The sun ascends, its tango spread,
Across the canvas wide,
In golden hues and rosy red,
The colors all collide.

The day departs with amber glow,
A symphony of light,
Encore of afterglow's soft show,
Before the fall of night.

In cycles of the dawn and dusk,
Eternal flames revolve,
The rhythms in the radiance, brusk,
In daylight's dance dissolve.

Viola's Verse

Upon a bed of velvet green,
The viola finds her tune,
In lavender and gold she's seen,
Beneath the crescent moon.

Her petals sway, a textured chord,
The garden's tranquil lay,
Each note she blooms in sweet accord,
Throughout the brightening day.

A solo in the silent hush,
As twilight's curtain falls,
She whispers in the gentle brush,
Her verse in nightfall calls.

Viola's tender serenade,
With dusk's soft cloak unfurled,
Plays on until the colors fade,
Into the quiet world.

The Chromatic Bard

Upon the canvas of the world so wide,
A chromatic bard, with brush in stride,
Paints the stories, hue by hue,
In the spectrum of the morning dew.

Across the valleys, mountains steep,
Through fields where wildflowers sleep,
Each stroke imbues life with grace,
As melodies of color embrace.

In every heart, the colors spill,
From the palette that his hands will,
To craft a world so vivid, so bright,
Soaring up on a rainbow's flight.

And when the twilight shadows start,
The bard retreats, his poetic art,
Leaves echoes on the skies just above,
A symphony in colors of love.

Echoes in Color

Whispers softly tread the air,
In shades of azure, light and fair,
Echoes dance in brilliant array,
As color speaks where words can't sway.

The crimson echo of a rose,
As the twilight of day gently dozes,
Silver whispers from the moon so bold,
In midnight tales that have yet to be told.

The golden murmur of the sun's descent,
Paints a path where day is spent,
Verdant echoes in the forest deep,
Hold secrets that the earth does keep.

And in the echoes, we find our place,
A spectrum of feelings interlaced,
In colors heard and deeply felt,
Within the echoes where hearts have dwelt.

Palette of Prose

With a palette of prose and vibrant themes,
An artist wordsmith weaves his dreams,
Each sentence a shade, each word a line,
Creating a masterpiece through time.

The artistry of language, bold and free,
Crafting visions for the world to see,
In the hues of imagination's glow,
A literary spectrum begins to flow.

Splash of passion, brush of grief,
Layered textures of belief,
Mixed on the palette with skill and care,
Words that color the blank air.

In this prose, a life is told,
Stories in shades of amber and gold,
A portrait drawn with eloquent ease,
Canvas of language, meant to please.

Whispering Tints

In the hushed silence of dawning light,
The whispering tints speak their might,
Softly coloring the break of day,
With the pastel words they say.

The tender green of new life's song,
Where the whispering tints belong,
They murmur in the breeze's play,
In every leaf along the way.

A murmur of blue in the ocean's depth,
Telling tales of the waves' breadth,
With each crest, the colors bend,
In whispers only the sea can send.

The gentle touch of twilight's grace,
As shades of dusk gently lace,
The sky listens to the fading light,
In the whispering tints of night.

Sestina Spectra

A tapestry of hues unfold in verse,
In woven words of green, blue, and red,
A poet's palette bleeds from day to night,
Complex patterns in the spectrum dance.

Echoes of the ancient form breathe life,
Within the sestet's disciplined embrace.
Each stanza spills its colors on the page,
Spectra twine through every sestina's grace.

Through every line, a fresh hue meets the eye,
Bright as the threads of dawn's first breaking light,
Six words repeat in symphonic array,
In the artful spectrum of poetic might.

End words cycle, a prismatic spin,
Six lines, six stanzas, a concluding tryst,
An envoy of three lines to tie the end,
In the sestina's spectra, none resist.

Couplet Chromatics

Lines paired in twos, like colors of the sky,
Couplets paint a picture smooth and bright.

Rhymes that chime like rainbows spreading wide,
Brush strokes of couplet chromatics alight.

Pairs in tune, with harmony's own sigh,
Verses dressed in evening's gentle light.

Nestled words, a dual chromatic flight,
Dancing hues, in couplet's canvas tight.

Cascades of Metaphor

Beneath the canopy of azure thought,
Waterfalls of imagery descent,
Rushing, gushing over craggy wit,
Cascades of metaphor without relent.

Each ripple sings a concept freshly caught,
Ideas in the mist are heaven-sent,
Sprays of creativity anoint,
As verses flow, new tributaries bent.

In the white water rush of poet's dream,
Language leaps like salmon to the sea,
Metaphors abound in liquid streams,
Infusing life with lingual ecstasy.

So metaphors cascade without a dam,
Churning through the caverns of the mind,
Forging rivers deep where thoughts can swim,
Within the poet's soul, they're intertwined.

Verses in Spectrum

In the realm where verses hold the light,
Each color finds its voice and sings aloud,
The spectrum spins, a carousel of words,
In every hue, the verses are endowed.

Reds ignite the passion of the night,
Yellows drench the dawn in golden shroud,
Blues serenade the slowly fading light,
And greens emerge in spring, in life avowed.

Purples dress the twilight in its might,
Oranges spill in sunsets boldly proud,
Every shade and tint adds to the delight,
A poet's canvas, vast and unavowed.

In poetic hues that spectrum gleams,
Verses carry forth the soul's bright beams,
Rainbow arcs where dreams are not just dreams,
In the spectrums of verse, the spirit deems.

Odes in Opal

In twilight's hush, the sky bestows,
A canvas smeared with opal glow,
The zephyrs whisper, soft and slow,
In rhymes that only nightfall knows.

Gentle tints of moon's embrace,
Drape the world in lustrous lace,
Each pale hue finds its own space,
In the hallowed evening's grace.

Stars like flecks on canvas vast,
Each a dream from heavens cast,
Opal skies, to nights affixed,
In tranquil verses are transmixed.

Silent ode to time’s soft flow,
Where thoughts in opal waters row,
The tranquil gleam, the gentle show,
As night performs its silent glow.

The Poet’s Palette

With words as paints, and mind the brush,
The poet strokes the silence, hush,
Dipping in emotion's rush,
On canvas of the heart's lush crush.

Verbs in vibrant violets swirl,
Adjectives like pearls unfurl,
Nouns in naked truth are hurled,
Adverbs twist as thoughts unfurl.

Metaphors in colors bleed,
Similes like sunflowers seed,
Each stanza grows from idea’s feed,
A blooming garden from a single deed.

In the poet’s palette, hues combine,
To render feelings so divine,
In shades that thoughts and dreams entwine,
A masterpiece through lines benign.

Serenade in Cerulean

Upon the canvas of the day,
A cerulean serenade does play,
In waves of tranquil blues it lay,
As skies perform in calm ballet.

The sea reflects the azure song,
Where dolphins dance and swim along,
The horizons stretch, inviting, long,
In the hue where hearts belong.

Birdsong weaves through sapphire air,
A symphony of flight, so fair,
Each feather strokes the daydreams there,
In cerulean whispers shared.

Serenade of a balmy breeze,
Carrying blue notes with such ease,
Caressing days like soft appease,
In melodies the soul to please.

Rhyme's Rainbow Reverie

In rhymes resplendent, colors bend,
A rainbow's arch, the heavens lend,
A spectrum scribed to hearts commend,
Each hue in verse doth gently wend.

Reds in romance gently fare,
Oranges laughter in the air,
Yellows shine in the sunny glare,
Greens grow in meadows fair.

Blues serenade the dreamy sky,
Indigos whisper their deep-sigh,
Violets bloom in twilight's eye,
In unity, their arcs ally.

Each color paints a different dream,
Together in poetic scheme,
A rainbow reverie, it seems,
In the tapestry of themes.

Tints of Tones

In whispered hues of twilight song,
Beneath the moon’s soft, silver throng,
Vibrations dance, the air along,
In tints of tones where dreams belong.

Tender is the night’s embrace,
Soothing shades in gentle grace,
Melodies that interlace,
In serenade’s harmonious space.

Echoes float in the cool, dark air,
A symphony of shades laid bare,
Moments colored beyond compare,
In the orchestra of nighttime's fare.

Each whisper sings a colored light,
Harmonies in varied flight,
Tones that chase away the night,
With every hue comes new delight.

Lyric's Luminance

Words glow with a melody's fire,
Ignited by the heart's own pyre,
Each line burns brighter, higher,
In lyric's dance, a burning choir.

Verse like candles in the mind,
Shadows retreat where they find,
Luminous thoughts gently twined,
In golden threads of the enshrined.

Stirring rhythms cast their blaze,
Upon the thoughts, the soul's gaze,
Lyric's luminance softly plays,
In the mind's eye, a brilliant maze.

Brightly shine the spoken streams,
In cascades of enlightened dreams,
Lines alight with glowing beams,
In flowing ink, the spirit gleams.

Palette of Prose

Brushstrokes of sentiment on white,
Coloring darkness with words alight,
A canvas rich with shades so bright,
In palette of prose, our hearts write.

Dabs of emotion in every hue,
Stories painted old and new,
Words that dip in morning dew,
Prose painted in every view.

Literary landscapes come to life,
Beyond the realm of any strife,
Artful letters cut like a knife,
Through the canvas, sharp as a fife.

In mosaics of metaphors and similes,
Written rainbow breathes and frees,
The artist's touch that none can seize,
In the gallery of written ease.

Stanza Silhouettes

Silent figures drawn in lines,
Poetry's shadow softly refines,
Glimpses of tales through the confines,
In stanza silhouettes, meaning entwines.

Contoured shapes in the text's twilight,
Carved from words in the deep night,
Figures that dance without a light,
In the poem’s dim, a reader’s delight.

Silhouettes of love, loss, and lore,
Stories told in the rhythm’s core,
Outlines that both soothe and soar,
In the verse’s quiet, its silent roar.

Each silhouette, a tale to unveil,
In language's shadow, concepts regale,
Stanzas tell their own quiet tale,
In poetic forms, they never pale.

Sonnet Shadows

In twilight hues, the whispered sonnet fades,
As shadows stretch to claim the day's last light,
Each silhouette a stanza, softly laid,
Upon the parchment of the coming night.

In depths of darkness, secrets are composed,
With lines of longing, scribed in silver glow,
These sonnet shadows, gracefully imposed,
Reveal the heart's truth only stars may know.

The dusk intones a sonnet's soft lament,
A cadence carried on the cool night breeze,
In nightfall's cloak, the day's loud voice is spent,
And sonnets find their tranquil harmonies.

When dawn returns to break the shadow's thrall,
The sonnet shades in morning light dissolve.

Echoes of the Muse

Echoes of the muse resound through time,
Inspiring hearts with rhythm and with rhyme,
Their whispers weave through every poet's mind,
Guiding pens to write what souls unwind.

In silent rooms where thought and fancy blend,
A symphony of echoes then descend,
From ancient tales to sonnets yet unspun,
The muse's echoes dance from sun to sun.

The muse's voice, a timbre pure and clear,
Resonates in those who hold her near,
In echoed halls where every word's a seed,
These echoes of the muse fulfill our need.

When words fall silent, and the ink runs dry,
The muse's echoes never truly die.

Rhyme's Refraction

Through rhyme's refraction, light bends into verse,
In prism'd lines where colors merge and part,
The spectrum of the soul, both bright and terse,
Reflects the varied hues of human heart.

Each couplet casts a shade distinct and bold,
The meter bends, a dance of light and sound,
With rhymes that break and blend like beams of gold,
A brilliant burst of life in words is found.

The poet's craft, to bend the beam of thought,
Through rhyme’s clear crystal, splitting light to lines,
The beauty that refracted rhyme has wrought,
In each new reading, differently it shines.

Within the poem’s glass, a world refracts,
In endless rhymes, life’s spectrum interacts.

Odes to Opacity

Odes to opacity, anthems obscure,
Celebrate mystery, praise the unclear,
Verses that venture where sight does not dare,
In ambivalent words, their meanings ensnared.

They dance in the shadows of doubt and belief,
Where light meets the dark, and relief meets grief,
The dense lines of poetry, thick with intrigue,
Confounding the certain, the ode's own league.

In opaque waters of poetic flows,
Clarity's current seldom shows,
Yet in that depth, truth often hides,
And in enigma, wisdom abides.

Give praise to the vague, to the unseen the toast,
For in opaque odes, depth may linger most.

Tones of Tempest

Upon the furious tempest's roar,
Raging winds that keenly score,
Waves that clash in wild debate,
Nature's fury we contemplate.

Gales that tear through tattered sails,
Mighty storms that time assails,
Thunder's drum, the lightning's lance,
In this chaos, spirits dance.

Spirits whisper in the squall,
Heeding to the tempest's call,
The ocean's heart, it pounds and heaves,
In the storm, our fear it weaves.

Yet within the tumult's song,
Strength and courage are born strong,
Tempest's tones may fiercely blare,
But bring to life a brave affair.

Shadows in Verse

In the quiet gloom they wait,
Silent authors of my fate,
Verses veiled in darkened hues,
Shadows whispering their muse.

Each line a specter of the night,
Crafting song without the light,
In the black, their tales unfold,
Stories in the dark, they're told.

Echoes of a hidden pain,
In their silence, much is gained,
Words that dance with somber grace,
Leaving not a single trace.

Yet, these verses that I find,
In the shadows of my mind,
Hold the truth within their grip,
As from my pen, they slowly slip.

Saturated Sonnets

Verses soaked in hues so deep,
Colorful secrets that they keep,
In saturated lines they speak,
Of loves lost, and the strength we seek.

Each sonnet a vivid dream,
In the pools of thought, they teem,
Drenched in passion's heavy rain,
Words that wash away the pain.

With every rhyme, a hue is cast,
In the sonnet's die is cast,
The palette of the poet's heart,
From the canvas, will not part.

So let these drenched sonnets flow,
In their richness, let us grow,
For in these lines, we find our lot,
In saturated verses caught.

Decanting Desires

Pour out the vintage of longing concealed,
Beneath the cork, emotions unsealed,
With each drop that spills, desires reveal,
In the decanting, our hearts we heal.

Swirl gently the glass of yearning claret,
Unveil the bouquet of dreams to harriet,
In its crimson depths, our wishes beget,
A vintage of hope, in sunsets we're set.

Tannins of truth in the soul's carafe,
Sipping on futures, with each draft we quaff,
Decant our dreams, let them take shape and staff,
In the liquid dance, our spirits, they laugh.

Desires, in vessels of clarity pore,
Fulfillment's bouquet we seek to explore,
Uncorked ambitions, we not ignore,
Decanted, our longings forevermore.

Ballade of the Blue

Beneath the boundless sky so vast and blue,
A whispering ocean echoes its hue,
Where dreams take flight on seas so true,
Under the canvas of a color so pure and due.

The midnight moon spills secrets to the dew,
With starry tales dipped in the darkest brew,
Silent thoughts in the blue depths grew,
A serenade to the night's enchanting view.

Azure waves dance with the wind's cue,
Harmony in the blue, an artists' retinue,
Shades melding where seagulls flew,
Singing the ballade of the blue, ever anew.

In the serene blue, our lives we construe,
In layers of sapphire, we find our clue,
Living, breathing in the eternal blue,
Enshrined forever, in the ballade's gentle imbue.

Vermilion Vernacular

With a brush dipped in vermilion fire,
Words ignite with passionate desire,
The canvas speaks in tones higher,
Painting language in red attire.

Vermilion verses sing in a choir,
Their voice a burning, fervent lyre,
Each sentence alight, an ardent spire,
In the vernacular of a flame that will never tire.

A poet's pen, a glowing wire,
Vermilion vernacular, a love transpire,
Burning bright, it's a beacon's pyre,
Words that in their warmth, inspire.

In the heart's deep corners to inquire,
There lies the vermilion vernacular's empire,
In vivid hues, our thoughts respire,
The fiery speech of the soul's aspire.

Rainbow Rhyme Revue

In the sky, a bow of light anew,
A tapestry with every vibrant hue,
On raindrops, the sun's ray slew,
Birthing a revue of colours so true.

Red whispers to the orange a soft ado,
Yellow giggles with green without clue,
Blue syncs with indigo, a deeper preview,
Violet serenades the mix, a harmonic coup.

Rainbow Rhyme, a spectacle to view,
A lyrical dance, a poetic brew,
Each shade with a verse, a dazzling queue,
Words that sparkle like morning dew.

As the sun bows and the sky turns to twilight's pew,
The Rainbow Rhyme ends in the night's venue,
But in dreams, those colours continue to break through,
In the revue, we remember life's vibrant tattoo.

Silver Streak Sonnets

A streak of silver in the twilight sky,
Stars like diamonds, a time to sigh,
Moon's soft glow, a lullaby,
Whispered sonnets in the night's reply.

Shadows cast in the silver dye,
Mysteries unraveled by the moon's spy,
Every sonnet, a secret tie,
Moments captured where dreams comply.

Silver light, the night's ally,
Guiding poets as they try,
To paint in words, an immortal why,
In sonnets that soar and never die.

In the silver streak, our hearts identify,
A truth within the celestial high,
The sonnets speak as the hours fly,
In the silver glow, we find reply.

Monochrome Melodies

Silent shades whisper in light and dark,
Canvas bare, yet full, a silent park.
Each hue sings a note so stark,
In monochrome melodies that leave their mark.

Sketches formed in blacks and grays,
Harmonies composed in unseen ways.
A symphony of contrast, the eye surveys,
In this muted world where the raven brays.

No spectrum here, just scale refined,
In simplicity, a complex design.
Each stroke, each shadow entwined,
An achromatic sonnet, exquisitely lined.

From the abyss to the purest white,
Each gradient dances with delight.
Monochrome melodies, devoid of spite,
In the absence of color, a different light.

Saffron Stanzas

Amber hues lace the morning beam,
Saffron tales from a daydream dream.
Threads of sunlight gently stream,
Weaving warmth in a golden gleam.

Spicy whispers on the breeze,
A scent, a colour; to seize and please.
In every verse it's ease and tease,
Saffron stanzas crafted to appease.

A field where marigolds sway and dance,
Their color the essence of romance.
In these lines, they advance,
Golden garment stanzas in a trance.

A tinge that brightens the somber mood,
Vivid stanza, in festive food.
The joyful color of multitude,
Saffron shades of quietude.

Splashed in Splendor

A canvas kissed by a rainbow's end,
Colors burst, curve, and descend.
Pigments dance, blend, and mend,
A masterpiece life did commend.

Droplets flung with a painter's pride,
Hues that swirl and never hide.
In every dash, nature's stride,
The spectrum's width, fully applied.

Verdant green and ocean blue,
A floral burst of every hue.
Nature's brush does imbue,
Splendor splashed in morning dew.

Enchantment lies where colors splash,
In every stroke, a dreamland's dash.
Under the sun's luminous flash,
Life becomes a vibrant sash.

Fiery Fuchsia Phrases

Fuchsia blooms in vibrant verse,
A color so loud, it might just curse.
Each line a petal, or perhaps inverse,
A bold statement, no need to rehearse.

Phrases woven with passionate fire,
Words that resonate with desire.
In this hue, emotions aspire,
Fiery phrases that never tire.

This poem bleeds a bright magenta,
A fervent heart, the center's placenta.
Each stanza's a bloom, a fiery agenda,
In fuchsia tones, a warm epicenter.

A rhapsody written in radiant flux,
Where roses and rhymes intermix.
Fuchsia phrases not for the orthodox,
They blaze and burn, a poetic crucifix.

Eloquent Emerald Emissions

In forests deep where shadows play,
Emerald leaves emboss the day,
Softly gleaming, whispers fade,
Nature's silent serenade.

Jeweled tones in velvet swells,
Stories that the earthshell tells,
Dappled light through canopies,
Gossamer threads in gentle breeze.

Unseen emissions, gems unseen,
Carpeting the ground in green,
Elegant in pure repose,
Nature's poem, perfectly composed.

Quiet whispers in the glen,
Chorus of the forest then,
Eloquent in emerald light,
Harmony's hue enchants the night.

Poetry in Pigments

Brush strokes on the canvas dance,
A prismatic, vibrant trance,
Reds and blues in tender fight,
Painting day, surrendering to night.

A ballet of hues in splendid array,
Each pigment with a novel say,
Sunset's fire, twilight's kiss,
Moments captured, pure bliss.

Ochre whispers to azure skies,
An artist's dream before the eyes,
Spectrum’s sonnet, silent delight,
Poetry in pigments, burning bright.

Canvas speaks in silent verse,
In each color, a universe,
Art's sweet resonance takes flight,
In the quiet gallery's tranquil light.

Luminous Lexicon

Words are lanterns in the night,
Beacons burning, oh so bright,
Phrases twirling, in their flight,
Conveying darkness, birthing light.

Letters strung like pearls so fine,
Narratives neatly intertwine,
Tapestries of thought align,
In the luminous lexicon define.

Stanzas shimmer, polished gold,
Stories braver, tales bold,
Poet's treasury, manifold,
Luminance within the fold.

Syntax ignites the silent stage,
In the spotlight, wisdom's sage,
Luminous lexicon, wise and brave,
Dancing on the page's ageless grave.

Marbled Muse Musings

In swirls of thought, my muse does play,
On marbled mindscape, abstract fray,
Idea's veining, rich and vast,
Timeless questions that we ask.

Through corridors of consciousness,
Past columns of sheer thoughtfulness,
Inspiration's palace rise,
Marbled halls beneath the skies.

Streaks of genius, slips of fate,
On the sculptor's mind they skate,
Figures carved in mental stone,
In the gallery of the great unknown.

Eddies of a musing dream,
Past realities' seam,
In marbled muse, imagination gleams,
Through the whispers of the artistic stream.

Shades of Verse

Whispers dance on a silent stage,
Beneath the ink, emotions rage.
Wisps of thought in the shadow's tune,
In the heart of night, under the moon.

Quiet hues of somber thought,
Crafting worlds from the battles fought.
Gentle grays paint soft decree,
In the shades of verse, we are free.

Dusky lines in twilight's keep,
Where secrets and silent muses meet.
A canvas vast, a boundless deep,
In verses' shades, our souls speak.

Ebon whispers of a muted plea,
The quill moves on determinedly.
Within the pen, pure truth resides,
In shades of verse, our spirit hides.

Chromatic Cadences

Red are the roses in verses anew,
Bleeding emotions, both fervent and true.
Cadences rise in a crimson flood tide,
Where passion and poetry equally reside.

Azure enchantment in each couplet flows,
Serenity whispers where the river prose goes.
Sapphire symphonies, harmonious light,
Chromatic cadences dance through the night.

Golden are the rhymes in verses that gleam,
Radiant and bright, like a sunbeam dream.
Every stanza glitters with prosperous hues,
A trove of the treasures that bards will choose.

Verdant are the lines with a life so lush,
Nature's own rhythm, in a soft-spoken hush.
Green-tinted echoes of a vibrant verse,
Chromatics embraced in the poet's universe.

Metaphor's Spectrum

On Metaphor's Spectrum, the colors collide,
Similes, images, vividly described.
Each idiom's a hue, distinct in its right,
Painting perception with linguistic light.

Visions of azure, that hint at the day,
Metaphors meander, in their abstract way.
Crimson-tales flicker, within this broad band,
Imagery's spectrum, at the poet's hand.

Emerald ideas sprawl, across the verse expanse,
Comparisons grow like leaves, given the chance.
Phrases unfurl in a kaleidoscope's dream,
Within metaphor's spectrum, concepts are the theme.

On the arc of the abstract, the colors they blend,
Figurative language, on which we depend.
Nuances flourish in radiant array,
In metaphor's spectrum, we find our way.

Lyrical Light

Within the stanzas, shines lyrical light,
Streaking through darkness, beaming and bright.
Each line a ray where glimmers ignite,
Casting a glow, through rhythm's night.

Words flicker like flames, in poetic fire,
Burning through silence, igniting desire.
Melodies woven in a tapestry so tight,
Lyrical light, fueling the flight.

Shadows shrink back as the verses grow warm,
With the heat of emotions, they take their form.
Light filters softly through the cracks of the heart,
Verse illuminates where whispers can start.

Dance in the beams of this incandescent script,
In the brilliance of song, we momentarily drift.
A beacon of hope in the ink's gentle might,
Forever we cherish the lyrical light.

Sonnet of Hues

In twilight's gentle grasp, soft colors blend,
A tapestry of shade shifts in the sky,
Each hue whispers the day's approaching end,
The azure realm kissed by amber goodbye.

The verdant trees in silhouette repose,
As evening paints with a cooler lave,
Night's curtain falls, the vivid scene it cloaks,
In restful darkness, all colors behave.

Yet soon the dawn will break in splendor bright,
And coax the hidden colors back to dance,
The sun's caress will wake the warmth of light,
Inciting day in a chromatic trance.

The cycle turns, the hues rotate the sphere,
The sonnet of colors always near.

Dappled Rhyme Rhapsody

Upon the canvas of the copse dappled light,
With mottled shade in playful hide and seek,
Nature's notes in whimsical meters take flight,
Composing a rhapsody unique.

Each rustling leaf a stanza does compose,
The wind, the maestro with a steady beat,
A symphony in the woods subtly grows,
A dappled rhyme where shadow and sunlight meet.

Sunbeams filter through the canopy breaks,
Complementing the chorus of the birds,
Nature's orchestra, no error it makes,
In the woodland, a rhapsody is heard.

Dappled light and rhyme dance hand in hand,
Together they play, together they stand.

Stanzas of Saturation

Drenched in color, each petal and leaf,
A saturation deep, the eye to feast,
Each shade to the soul does whisper relief,
In the garden, nature's vibrant masterpiece.

With every drop of rain, the colors sigh,
The wet world sings in tones so lush, so pure,
As if the earth indulged in a paint dye,
The hues intense, the saturation sure.

Fields of blossoms in radiant attire,
The artist's palette sprawled beneath the skies,
Each stroke and tint, a visual quire,
A sonnet spun from color's sweet reprise.

So drink in deep, this saturation bold,
The world's true colors, a sight to behold.

Lyrical Light Refraction

In prisms of light where secrets unveil,
The spectrum leaps forth, freed from its tight grasp,
Each band of color tells its own tale,
In lyrical light, the world does clasp.

The rainbow arcs in splendid high refrain,
Its colors sing in harmonious light,
A bridge of wonder, no need to explain,
The sky's lyrical score, pure and contrite.

Through droplets suspended, the sun's rays bend,
A visual chorus in the air aloft,
Light and water in a waltz without end,
Soft hues refract in whispers sweet and soft.

Bask in the ballet of light's reflection,
Nature's own lyrical light connection.

Quill and Quasar

Beneath the ink-black sky so vast,
A quasar's heart, in pulses cast.
With quill in hand, I scribe the night,
Transcribing cosmos burning bright.

Ancient light from far away,
Stories scribed in stellar play.
The quill dances with cosmic fire,
Capturing the universe's choir.

Galactic whispers gently sown,
In night's embrace, we're not alone.
Each stroke, a step in time's grand waltz,
Connecting dots, the stars' exalts.

Upon the parchment, time's tattoo,
Quill's legacy in heavenly hue.
The quasar's dance, forever shown,
In inky trails, the stars have sown.

Ballet in Blues and Beige

In a room where blues and beige entwine,
The dancers leap, their grace divine.
Softly woven, each pirouette and plié,
A symphony in motion, they convey.

The beige, a canvas for the blues' embrace,
The dancers' silhouettes move with grace.
Each step tells a story, rich and deep,
In the dance, their sorrows they unkeep.

Ballet in blues, a melancholic scene,
Beige shadows cast, a subtle sheen.
The dancers' hearts beat in tender merge,
While sorrow and joy, through movement, surge.

With elegance, they paint the air,
In blues and beige, a love affair.
Through every leap, spin, and glide,
They weave their stories, side by side.

Orphic Octaves in Onyx

In the depth of onyx night, I hear,
The Orphic octaves drawing near.
A chord struck from the underworld's lyre,
In shadows, music's somber choir.

The notes ascend in darkened scales,
A song of longing that never fails.
Each octave a rung on a ladder deep,
Where dreams and demons softly creep.

Resonance in the silent void,
The octaves' spell, not to be toyed.
A melody of mystic lore,
Haunting the heart's most secret core.

In the onyx night, the octaves play,
Orphic wisdom in dusky array.
With each tone, a tale is spun,
A symphony for the lost and won.

Incandescent Invocations

With words aflame, I light the dark,
Incandescent invocations, a fiery mark.
Summoning visions from the ember's glow,
The poem's power begins to grow.

Sparks leap to dance upon the page,
In the poet's hands, a burning sage.
Each phrase ignites the mind’s own eye,
A beacon in the blackened sky.

The stanza smolders, then takes flight,
An incantation in the depth of night.
Burning brighter with each verse,
In the poet's fire, the universe.

Embers of truth in each line's wake,
Passionate pleas for the soul to take.
In each glowing word, a fervent prayer,
Incandescent invocations fill the air.

Whispering Wavelengths

In silence, soft undulations bloom,
Echoes of the unseen tune,
Hushed tones through the ether zoom,
Carrying the light of the waning moon.

Waves that murmur to the night,
Bearing secrets in their flight,
A spectral dance of shade and light,
Whispers of the cosmos, out of sight.

Frequencies that faintly sigh,
In gentle breaths, they float by,
The stars, their hidden language ply,
In quiet conversation, sky to sky.

A symphony so still and deep,
In its embrace, the world does keep,
The humming earth in tranquil sleep,
These whispering wavelengths, forever to seep.

Sonorous Saturation

A symphony of colors loud,
In every hue, the world's endow'd,
The dawn spills in, a crimson shroud,
Piercing the skies, in brilliance bow'd.

Noon's blaze in azure spreads its claim,
A testament to daylight's flame,
Each moment, a new shade to name,
The land, a canvas, never the same.

Dusk's whispers adorned in gold,
Day's fiery heart begins to fold,
In cooling blues, night takes its hold,
A transition bold, in tones untold.

Through colors that in sound reside,
Visions that sing and coincide,
The eyes hear a rainbow wide,
In this sonorous saturation, we confide.

Epic's Eclat

Tales of old where legends dwell,
In every line, grand stories swell,
Heroic deeds and magic's spell,
Echo epic's eclat, a timeless yell.

Giants slain by hands so brave,
Lost kingdoms beneath the wave,
Mighty struggles that the fervent crave,
Carved in history, none can pave.

Journeys through the starlit breach,
To grasps at truths the wise beseech,
In every lesson, history's teach,
The echoes of an epic, in reach.

With each verse, a world's unfurled,
A tapestry of time is twirled,
Where valor's flag is high unfurled,
An epic's eclat, through ages hurled.

Pantoum Pigments

Painted whispers color the rhyme,
In pantoum patterns, shade and time,
Each line a thread, in design prime,
A tapestry of verse, so sublime.

In pantoum patterns, shade and time,
A repeat of hues, a mirrored climb,
A tapestry of verse, so sublime,
Cycling colors that chime.

A repeat of hues, a mirrored climb,
Strokes of memories, in pantoum's mime,
Cycling colors that chime,
The painter's touch in every line.

Strokes of memories, in pantoum's mime,
Painted whispers color the rhyme,
The painter's touch in every line,
Each line a thread, in design prime.

Printed in the USA
CPSIA information can be obtained
at www.ICGtesting.com
LVHW080609031223
765344LV00005B/90

9 789916 394731